# Mountains

## Jane & Steve Parker

### Consultant: Keith Lye

**FRANKLIN WATTS**
A Division of Grolier Publishing
NEW YORK • LONDON • HONG KONG • SYDNEY
DANBURY, CONNECTICUT

© Franklin Watts 1997

First American Edition 1998 by
Franklin Watts
A Division of Grolier
Publishing Co., Inc.
90 Sherman Turnpike
Danbury, Connecticut 06816

Library of Congress Cataloging-in-Publication Data

Parker, Jane, 1951–
    Mountains / Jane & Steve Parker.
       p.   cm. — (Take 5 geography)
    Includes index.
    Summary: An overview of the rich and varied environments of the earth's mountainous regions as exemplified by five of the most famous mountains in the world.
    ISBN 0–531–14457–7
    1. Moutnains—Juvenile literature.   [1. Mountains.]   I. Paker, Steve.  II. Title.  III. Series.
GB512.P368  1998
551.43'2—dc21

                                              97–20771
                                                 CIP
                                                    AC

Series editor: Kyla Barber
Designer: Ness Wood
Illustrator: Joanna Biggs
Picture researcher: Susan Mennell
Art director: Robert Walster
Consultant: Keith Lye

Printed in Great Britain

## Photographic credits:

t=top, b=bottom, c=center, l=left, r=right
Cover photo, Robert Harding, Thomas Laird
4, Royal Geographic Society, David Constantine;
5, Eye Ubiquitous, TMP/NASA;
7 l, Mountain Camera, John Warburton-Lee;
7 r, Bruce Coleman, John Shaw;
8, Images;
9 l, Planet Earth Pictures, Krafft;
9 r, Paul Popper;
10 l, James Davis Travel Photography;
10 r, Science Photo Library/Geospace;
11, Bruce Coleman., Hans-Peter Merten;
12, Mountain Camera, John Cleare;
13 l, Mountain Camera, John Cleare;
13 r, NHPA, Haroldo Palo Jr;
14, Oxford Scientific Films, Doug Allan;
15 l, NHPA, Daryl Balfour;
15 r, Bruce Coleman, Bauer;
16, Royal Geographic Society, Paul Harris;
17 l, Bruce Coleman, Hans Reinhard;
17 r, Bruce Coleman, Steven C Kaufman;
18, Mountain Camera, John Cleare;
19 l, Bruce Coleman, Rod Williams;
19 r, Bruce Coleman, Rinnie Van Meurs;
20 , Robert Harding Picture Library, Adina Tovy;
21 l, Bruce Coleman, Steven C Kaufman;
21 c, Mountain Camera, Tadashi Kajiyama;
21 r, e.t.archive, National Museum, Athens;
22, Eye Ubiquitous, J Burke;
23 t, Bruce Coleman, Staffan Widstrand;
23 b, James Davis Travel Photography;
24, Royal Geographic Society, Stephen Venables;
25 l, James Davis Travel Photography;
25 r, Royal Geographic Society;
26, Oxford Scientific Films, Colin Monteath;
27 l, Andes Press Agency, Carlos Reyes-Manzo;
27 r, James Davis Photography;
28, Bruce Coleman, Mary Plage;
29 l, Bruce Coleman, John Murray;
29 r, Mountain Camera, John Cleare.

## Contents

Tops of the World  4
Making Mountains  6
Mountains of Fire  8
Worn Away  10
Powerful Forces  12
Weather of the World  14
Tough at the Top  16
Ups and Downs  18
Mountain Spirits  20
Mountain People  22
Fun in the Mountains  24
Mountain Riches  26
Preserving Our Peaks  28

Glossary  30
Fact File  31
Index  32

# Tops of the World

Have you stood on a mountaintop and looked out over the landscape far below? It's a wonderful feeling to be so high and to gaze far and wide. Mountains have fascinated people since ancient times. They are mysterious haunts of monsters and spirits, barriers to travelers, home to the world's most fascinating wildlife—and dangerous places to wander in and climb.

## Everchanging

Mountains form in various ways and, like the rest of Earth's surface, they are always changing. Some grow as great wrinkles and folds in Earth's rocky surface, thrown up by the incredibly powerful forces deep within the planet. Others build themselves as volcanoes. Still others are left standing as softer rocks around them are worn away.

*The 28 tallest mountains are all in the Himalayas and the adjoining Karakoram Range.*

## The highest place

The summit of Mount Everest is the highest place on our planet's surface. It towers 29,029 feet (about 8,854m) above sea level. And it's still growing, by about 2 inches (5cm) every year! Everest is one of hundreds of peaks in the mountain group, or range, called the Himalayas. This stretches from Afghanistan across northern India and Tibet to western China. The range is still being formed faster than it is worn away.

Mount Everest is not an isolated peak, towering above the lowlands. It is surrounded by hundreds of other snowy, windswept, jagged mountains that make up the Himalayas.

**Everest**: highest mountain on Earth; **Aconcagua**: highest mountain outside Asia.

FIVE WORLD MOUNTAINS

The five mountains featured in this book are spread around the world. The "flattest" landmass is Australia. Its tallest peak is Kosciusko, at 7,313 feet (2,229m).

## Take 5 Mountains

**Everest** (Nepal) is the world's highest peak, situated in the young and growing range of the Himalayas.

**Kilimanjaro** (Tanzania) is a tropical, extinct, and ancient volcano rising above the parched grasslands of Africa.

**Fuji** (Japan) is an ancient volcano, which has come to symbolize the culture and religion of a nation.

**Aconcagua** (Argentina) was a volcano caused by great movements of Earth's crustal plates, and it is the mysterious home to ancient spirits and civilisations.

**Loa** (Hawaii) is a fiery and unpredictable volcano, home to unique plants and animals.

### Higher than Everest?

Measured from bottom to top, Everest is not the world's tallest mountain. The record holder is Mauna Kea, on the island of Hawaii in the Pacific Ocean. It is 33,497 feet (10,217m) from its base deep on the seabed to the volcano at its summit.

And neither is the tip of Everest the farthest place from Earth's center. The peak of Mount Chimborazo in the Andes beats Everest by 7,054 feet (2,151m), because the planet is slightly pearshaped.

Some of the other planets in our galaxy have mountains, too. Highest of all is Mons Olympus on Mars. At about 82,000 feet, (25,010m) it's nearly three times taller than Everest!

**Kilimanjaro**: 19,230 feet (5,865m); **Mauna Loa**: 13,681 feet (4,173m); **Fuji**: 12,388 feet (3,778m).

# Making Mountains

Most mountains are called fold mountains because they are folds or wrinkles in Earth's crust—its solid, rocky outer layer. Peaks also form where huge blocks of rock crack along lines called faults, and get squeezed upward. These are called block-fault mountains.

## On the move

The surface of Earth seems unchanging. But the planet's outer "skin," the crust and the upper, rigid layer of the mantle, is made of about seven massive and other smaller slabs, called lithospheric plates. These float on a layer of incredibly hot, semimolten (runny) rock beneath called the mantle. Immense forces in the mantle push the plates above slowly around on the planet's surface, like a vast jigsaw. This gradual movement is called continental drift, because it makes the main landmasses wander around the planet.

## Big wrinkles

In some places, lithospheric plates are growing. Molten rock oozes up from the mantle and becomes solid, adding new crust to the edge of the plate. This happens mainly along chains of undersea mountains called oceanic ridges.

As the plates drift sideways, their opposite edges may press powerfully into neighboring plates. Slowly the solid rock bends, buckles, wrinkles, and folds. The result is a row or chain of fold mountains.

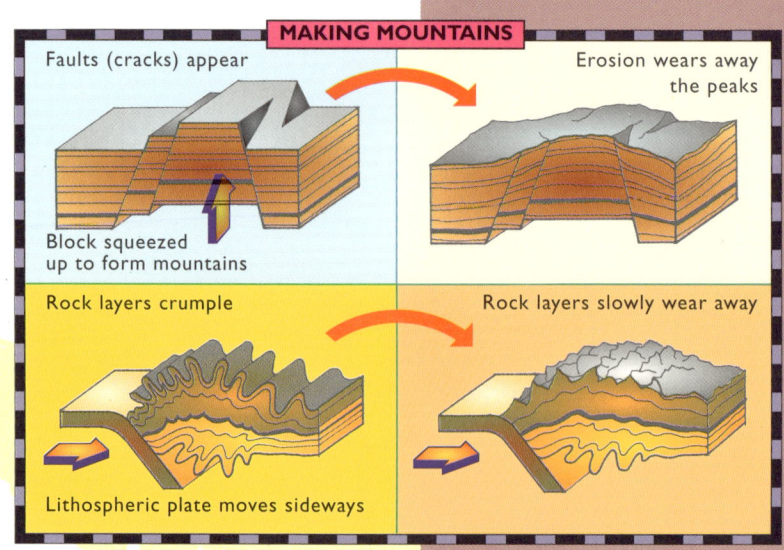

Rocks seem hard and unbending, but the immense forces of folding and faulting make them bend like cardboard or crack like dry wood.

**Everest**: the Himalayas are fold mountains, formed as two lithospheric plates collide.

## Old and new

The Andes are fold mountains, thrown up over the past 100 million years as the Nazca plate beneath the Pacific pressed into the South American plate. The highest peak in the Andes is Aconcagua in Argentina, at 22,864 feet (6,974m). The Himalayas and Alps are also fold mountains.

Aconcagua in the Andes cordillera in South America. The Andes mountain range is very long, 4,500 miles (7,245km), but only about 200 miles (322km) wide.

## Slow, then sudden

Continental drift and crustfolding are usually too slow to see. But sometimes the jagged edges of neighboring lithospheric plates get stuck. They cannot move or slide past each other, perhaps for centuries. Massive forces build up, stronger and stronger. Then, suddenly, the plates slip with a violent shock and shudder—an earthquake.

Earthquakes are a terrible and destructive side effect of the process of mountain building. They are most common in fold-mountain areas like the Andes and Himalayas and the many mountainous islands of Southeast Asia.

### Pikes Peak or bust!

Hard rocks such as granite form deep within Earth, where the pressure and temperature are colossal. These conditions also produce beautiful gemstones and nuggets of precious metals such as gold. Pike's Peak, in Colorado, U.S., is one of these massive lumps of ancient granite, formed as part of the Rocky Mountains, about 100 million years ago. Gold was discovered there in 1859. Wild West pioneers rushed to find their fortunes, crying "Pikes Peak or bust!"

Pikes Peak, in the Rockies, rises to 14,111 feet (4,304m). Today it is a popular tourist attraction.

**Aconcagua**: the Andes, also fold mountains, began to grow again two million years ago.

# Mountains of Fire

Most mountains take millions of years to form. But volcanoes may appear in just a few days. Molten rock, forced up by pressures beneath, spews out at Earth's surface.

Hot rocks in the volcanic crater of Mount St. Helens, Washington, smoke menacingly.

## Magma into lava

An erupting volcano is an awesome sight. Magma, molten rock from deep below, bursts up with incredible force through a weak spot in the crust. It emerges either as clouds of ash, or as lava, red hot and runny, destroying everything in its path.

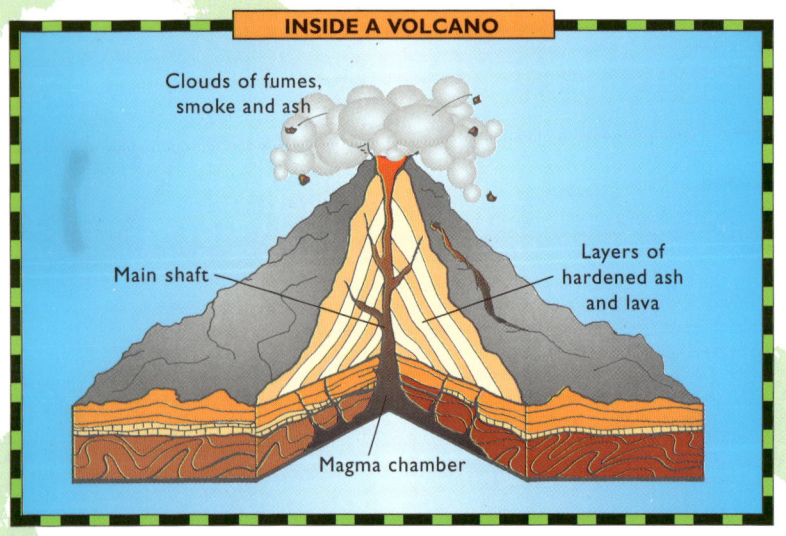

**INSIDE A VOLCANO**
- Clouds of fumes, smoke and ash
- Main shaft
- Layers of hardened ash and lava
- Magma chamber

## Layer by layer

Further eruptions pile on more lava. Layer by layer, a new mountain grows. Volcanoes erupt wherever Earth's crust is weak or stressed. This includes the edges of lithospheric plates, which is why fold mountains, volcanoes, and earthquakes often occur together.

**Mauna Loa**: its lava oozes and flows for more than 43 miles (69km).

## Hot spots

The Hawaiian Islands form a line in the Pacific Ocean, like beads on a necklace. This is not chance. Each island began as a volcano on the seabed, above a part of the mantle below, called a "hot spot." Each volcano erupted many times and formed an underwater mountain, or sea mount, the tip of which gradually grew above the waves.

## One after the other

As the lithospheric plate of the Pacific Ocean floor drifted northwest, a new part of it came above the Hawaiian hot spot. Another volcano built up another new island, which steamed and fizzed as it broke the sea's surface. This process continued, forming the chain of Hawaiian Islands over the past 25 million years.

### Global catastrophe

One of the greatest volcanic eruptions in recent history was in 1991. In the Philippines, Mount Pinatubo blasted out not much lava, but vast quantities of ash, dust, and smoke. The ash settled in a silent blanket over the surrounding area, destroying wildlife and buildings. The dust rose into the air, spread around the world, and affected global weather for two years.

Volcanic ash from Mount Pinatubo choked nearby towns.

Mauna Loa is the world's largest active volcano. Its lava flows glow red hot.

## Active island

As the first, oldest Hawaiian Islands drifted away from the volcanic area, they cooled and began to wear down. Today, the island of Hawaii itself is over the hot spot. It has two peaks. Mauna Kea is older and taller, at 13,796 feet (4,208m), and no longer erupts. Mauna Loa is 13,681 feet (4,173m) high, still active and growing. Near Mauna Loa is the Kilauea crater, which has been extremely active in recent years, emitting spectacular streams of lava.

**Fuji** is dormant, or "asleep." **Kilimanjaro** is probably extinct or "dead."

# Worn Away

Mountain building, or orogeny, started when Earth's crust cooled and turned to solid rock, about 4,000 million years ago. Many huge peaks have risen up since then. But most have been worn away by the forces of nature. The mountains existing today only appeared in the last few hundred million years.

## The power of weather

The rocks of Earth's crust cannot last forever. As shown on page 12, they are battered by rain, frozen by ice, blanketed by snow, blasted by wind and baked by the sun. These forces of weathering are especially powerful on high mountains. They crack and chip the rocky surfaces into small pieces. Rain washes the bits into streams and rivers. Gradually the mountain is worn away, or eroded.

This satellite photograph of the Himalayas shows their still high, sharp, snowcovered peaks and deep valleys. In 100 million years, they will have been worn lower.

## Sharp to smooth

Relatively young mountains, like Everest in the Himalayas and Aconcagua in the Andes, have not eroded very much. Their peaks are still high, sharp, and jagged. Older mountains, like the Altai in Russia and the Caledonians in Scotland, have been around for up to 500 million years. Erosion has made them lower, smoother, and more rounded.

After 500 million years, the Cambrian Mountains of Wales are mostly worn away.

**Everest:** melting Himalayan snow and ice feed the huge Ganges and Brahmaputra rivers.

## Dumped on the seabed

Where do the worn-away bits of mountains go? Most are carried by streams into larger rivers and eventually into the sea. For example, the Indus, Ganges, and Brahmaputra Rivers carry worn-away bits of the Himalayas to the Indian Ocean. These settle on the seabed as ever-thickening layers of sand, mud, clay, and other fine particles called sediment.

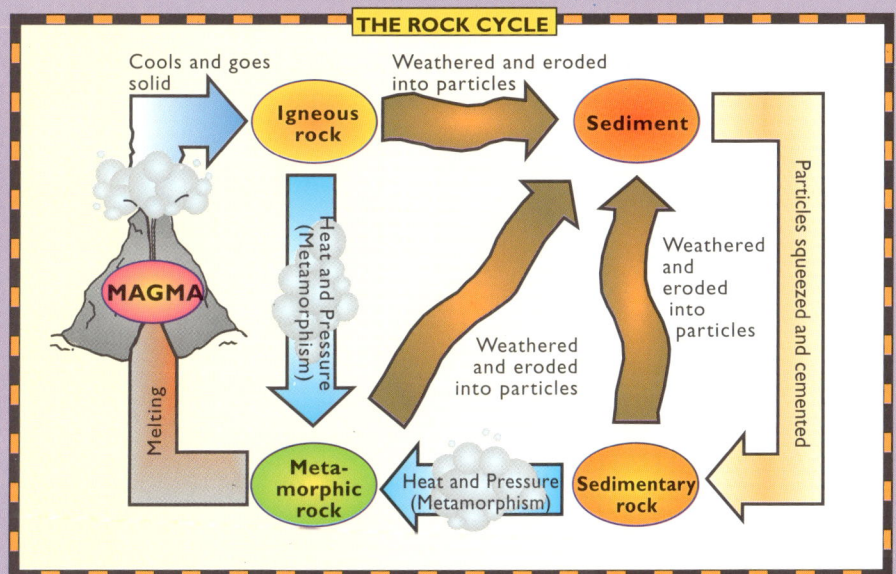

## The deadly Matterhorn

The Alps are Europe's highest and youngest mountain range. They are steep, sharp, and angular, hardly worn at all. The Matterhorn, on the border between Switzerland and Italy, is one of the highest peaks in the range, at 14,698 feet (4,483m). More climbers have died on its steep, slippery sides and towering cliffs than on any other mountain in the Alps.

The Matterhorn is a giant sharp-tipped pyramid of rock.

## The rock cycle

Over millions of years, the particles of sediments on the seabed are squeezed and solidified into solid rock. This rock might melt down into the mantle, and then emerge again as lava to form volcanic mountains. Or it could be buckled by Earth's movements into fold mountains. Or it could crack into gigantic blocks, which are then pushed upward by plate movement, forming block-fault mountains. In these various ways, rocks are eroded and then re-formed in a never-ending process called the rock cycle.

Every year, the Amazon River carries 350 million tons of eroded rock from the Andes out into the Atlantic Ocean.

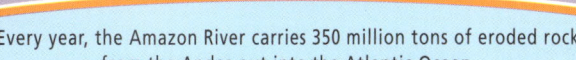

**Aconcagua**: sediments from the Andes cross South America in the Amazon River.

# Powerful Forces

The solid rocks of mountains are eroded by the forces of weathering. These are physical and chemical processes that crack, chip, and break rocks and stones into smaller pieces, which are washed away by rain or blown away by the wind.

## Running water

The fast-flowing water of a mountain stream rubs away rock, but very slowly. However, it also carries pebbles and stones that bounce along the stream bed, chipping off rocky fragments. Rainwater also contains tiny amounts of natural acids. These eat into the rock chemically, producing crevices and channels that weaken it. The extra acids in "acid rain," caused by pollution, greatly speed up this process.

In mountain areas like the Andes, fast rivers, such as the Rio Urubamba, soon wear away deep, steep, V-shaped valleys. They are fed by smaller streams rushing down from the highest slopes.

*The salt in today's seas and oceans came from the erosion of the first mountains on Earth, 4,000 million years ago.*

## Gouging glacier

On many mountains, ice and snow collect and flow very slowly downhill, as "ribbons of ice" called glaciers. These carry stones and boulders frozen into their undersides. They rub and gouge the rock beneath like giant sandpaper, wearing away rounded, U-shaped valleys.

**Everest**: the Himalayas have the world's deepest valley—it is 16,650 feet (5,078m).

# Expanding ice

Ice is a powerful weathering agent. When water seeps into tiny cracks in rock, and then freezes into ice, it gets bigger, or expands. This enlarges the crack and causes bits of rock to flake and chip off. This is called frost wedging.

A glacier slides slowly down a mountain valley, gouging the rock.

# Temperature and wind

The glaring sun beats down and heats the rock surface, making it expand. At night, the temperature drops and the rock contracts, or shrinks. This constant hot-cold cycle eventually cracks the surface of rocks, which peel away like the layers of an onion. Another weathering agent is wind. It picks up dust, sand, and other particles, and throws them against the mountainside like a massive sandblaster.

# Plant power

The slopes of lower mountains, like Fuji in Japan, are not brown but green. Plants grow, sending their roots into tiny crevices to search for nutrients, water, and anchorage. But as the roots grow, they open cracks and split the rock, causing yet more erosion.

## The frozen south

The rocky surface of the great southern continent, Antarctica, is covered by thick ice. Snow falls, becomes squeezed into ice, and slides slowly outward in all directions at about 33 feet (10 m) a year. It's like a giant circular glacier which erodes the land below—especially Antarctica's highest mountain, Vinson Massif at 16,864 feet (5,144m).

Antarctic glaciers rub away the rocks below, then spill into the sea.

**Kilimanjaro:** the lower slopes wear away fairly slowly, due to the mild tropical weather.

# Weather of the World

**Great mountain ranges are so big that they create their own weather—and they also have dramatic effects on the weather around the world. They bend winds, create clouds, shade the lowlands, and make rain fall.**

Clouds gather near a mountain peak—created by the presence of the mountain itself.

## Global patterns

The sun shines on Earth, heats different areas by different amounts, and causes the regular weather patterns, which we call climate. It's warm in the Tropics and cold at the Poles. Mountains are so huge that they interfere with these global patterns of temperature, sunshine, wind, rain, and snow.

*Temperatures fall by about almost a degree Fahrenheit for every 329 feet (100m) of height.*

## Rain and snow

Warm winds pass over the sea and take up moisture in the form of invisible water vapor. As they blow up a mountain slope, they cool and the water vapor condenses into tiny water droplets—clouds. The droplets join into drops and fall as rain. Higher still, where the temperature is even lower, rain turns to sleet and snow.

This is why mountains are often cold and shrouded in mist, clouds, and rain, when the nearby lowlands may be calm, dry, and sunny. The direction of the main winds makes one side of the mountain wet, while the other side is sheltered and drier. And coastal mountains with onshore winds, tend to have greater rainfall than mountains far inland.

*Weather at the top of Everest is extreme—temperatures often drop below -94°F (-70°C).*

Kilimanjaro's snowy and icy summit is far below freezing. About 2.5 miles (4km) below, warmth-loving animals such as zebras and lions thrive on the grasslands.

## Snow in the tropics

Mount Kilimanjaro, in Tanzania, is almost on the equator. Its summit, 19,341 feet (5,899m) high, is permanently covered with snow and ice. Yet the surrounding plains are hot and dry. This shows one main feature of mountain weather. The higher you go, the colder it gets, because the thin air cannot absorb and hold the sun's warmth. A peak of 3,280 feet (1,000m) is about 9°F cooler than the land around it. Winds also become stronger as you go up, especially in the first 3,280 feet (1,000m).

## Rainshadows

As winds blow over mountains, the rising air is cooled and the winds lose their moisture. When the winds descend on the other side of the mountain, the air gradually becomes warmer. The winds take up moisture from the land and there are few clouds and little rain. Many of the world's mountain ranges have rain-shadow dry regions on the downwind, or leeward, sides. Some even have deserts. The prairies of North America lie in the rain shadow of the Rocky Mountains.

### Mount McKinley

North America's highest peak is Mount McKinley, in Alaska. It is inside the Arctic Circle, and of its total height of 20,322 feet (6,198m), the topmost 13,100 feet (4,000m) are always covered with snow and glaciers. Mount Kilimanjaro is almost as tall, but it is in the warm Tropics. So only its topmost 6,562 feet (2,001m) are ice-covered.

Mount McKinley is blasted by winds of amore than 100 miles (161km) per hour.

Winds blast the peak at up to 192 miles per hour (309 kph).

# Tough at the Top

Plants and animals that live high in the mountains have to cope with harsh conditions. It's cold, windy, dull, damp, rough, and rocky, and breathing is difficult in the thin air. So the wildlife is specially adapted to cope with these problems. Each great range of mountains has its own unique selection of plants and animals.

Little survives in these harsh conditions.

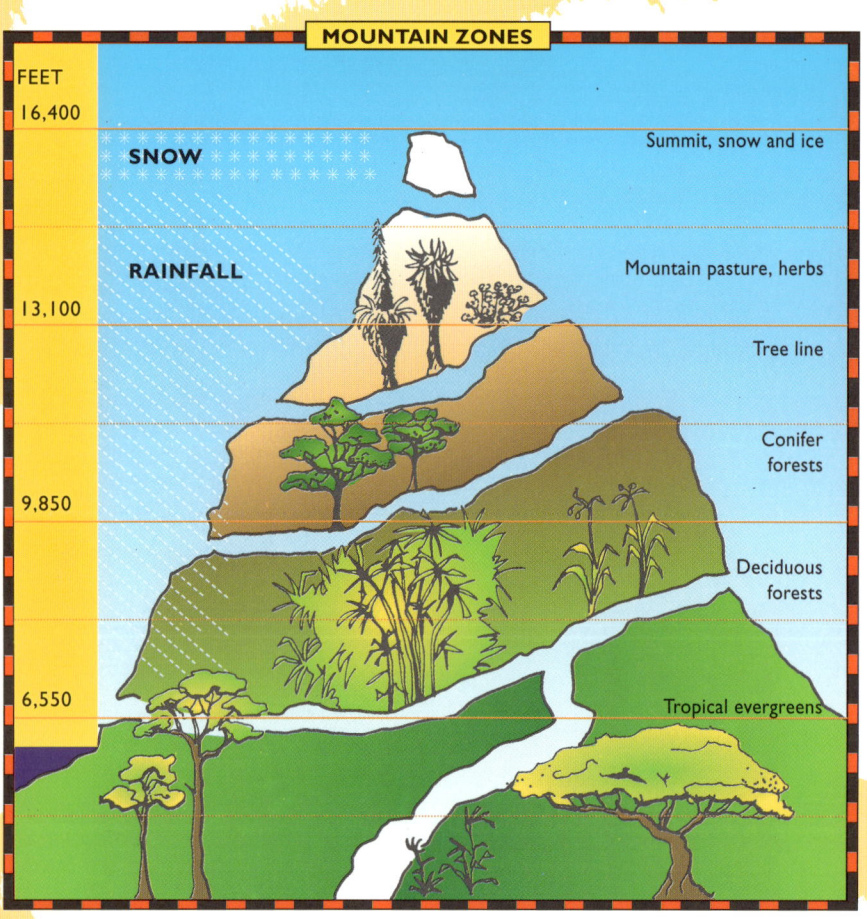

## The lowlands

To the east of the Northern Andes lie the Amazon rain forests. Tropical warmth and plentiful moisture encourage thousands of different plants, birds, insects, and other animals. It's the world's richest area for wildlife.

The fall in temperature up a mountain means different plants and animals are able to live at different altitudes.

Particular peak plants: **Everest**: hairy saussurea; **Aconcagua**: Antarctic pearlwort;

## The foothills

The Andean foothills are cooler, and tropical lowland rain forests of evergreen hardwood trees and brightly-colored parrots give way to subtropical cloud forests of palms and bamboo. There are fewer different species. Above the clouds grow trees that shed their leaves in the dry season.

## Conifers and grasses

Higher still are coniferous trees such as pines, firs, and spruces. They are better suited to the cooler, dry conditions. The upper edges of the forest mark the tree line, where woods give way to the next level or zone of vegetation—mountain meadows of grasses and herbs. Here and there an Andean puya, 33 feet tall (10m), towers above the pasture. This yucca like plant takes 100 years to flower, and then it dies.

Approaching the snow line, the plants become smaller. They grow close to the ground in cushion shapes, with tiny, hairy, wax-covered leaves that can withstand the icy winds.

The Hawaiian silversword is unique and specially adapted to its mountain home.

### The Rocky Mountains

The foothills of the Rockies are covered by sagebrush, juniper, and piñon. Grizzly and black bears, coyotes, and wolverines hunt in the higher forests of ponderosa and lodgepole pines, Douglas fir, and aspen. Farther up, mountain goats and bighorn sheep wander the alpine meadows of flowers and grasses. Even the ice fields of the peaks have wildlife, including mites, spiders, grasshoppers, and other insects.

Brown bears in the Rocky Mountains.

## Living in layers

Like the plants, the animals live in layers, or zones of altitude. Many have thick coats of fur or feathers to keep out the cold. The mountain vizcacha can survive living in rock crevices as high up as 16,404 feet (5,003m). Small birds like the Andean diucas keep close to the rock surface and huddle together in flocks to keep warm. Above, Andean condors soar on the mountain winds.

**Kilimanjaro:** giant groundsel; **Mauna Loa:** silversword; **Fuji:** rhododendron.

# Ups and Downs

Some mountain animals stay in the same place throughout the year. Insects and spiders survive by laying eggs that can withstand the icy cold of winter, hidden in plants or crevices. But some of the larger creatures travel up and down the slopes with the seasons, to find food and shelter and avoid predators.

## Regular travels

Like all main mountain ranges, the Himalayas have different climate zones at different altitudes, each with its unique plants and animals. But some creatures travel regularly, or migrate, up and down their mountains with the seasons.

Himalayan snow cocks have grey and white feathers, to blend in with the patches of snow and bare rock—or snow and bare bark. During the cold winter, they shelter in the high forests just below the tree line, among the snow-covered rhododendrons, junipers, and birch trees. In the warmth of early spring, they fly up to the mountain meadows. These soon become rich in grasses, flowers, and herbs. Here the snow cocks nest and raise their chicks, before migrating down again to the trees in the autumn.

## Nimble leapers

In mountainous Europe and the Middle East, chamois make similar seasonal journeys. In summer they graze on the short grasses and herbs of the high alpine pastures. As winter approaches they descend to the conifer forests and eat mosses, lichens, and pine shoots. Thick fur keeps them warm, and soft, spongy hoof pads grip the slippery rocks.

The black yak is a wild form of cowlike creature. It has a long, thick, hairy coat to keep warm.

Big mammals on mountains: **Everest:** snow leopard and yak; **Aconcagua:** vicuna.

The snow leopard, or ounce, of the Himalayas is one of the world's rarest big cats.

## High-altitude hunters

As plant-eating animals migrate, hunting animals follow them. The rare snow leopard of the Himalayas prowls above the tree line, looking for snow cocks and other birds, and mammals such as ibex and wild sheep. In winter it follows these prey into the high forests. Many types of medium and small cats prey on birds and small mammals in the Andes. They include the well-named Andean mountain cat.

Large birds can fly up a mountain in minutes. The huge lammergeier vulture dwells from the Alps to the Himalayas. It soars on the mountain wind, looking for bones and bits of dead animals. It picks up a bone in its beak, flies high, drops the bone to smash on the rocks, then eats the nutritious marrow inside.

### Unique wildlife

Mount Cook, 12,349 feet (3,766m) tall, is the highest peak in New Zealand. Its plants and animals are very unusual, not only because they live on a mountain, but also because this mountain is on an island that became separated from other lands over 100 million years ago! Famous flightless birds, the kiwi and kakapo (a type of parrot), live in the forests around Mount Cook.

The kea is a large member of the parrot family that scavenges in the mountains of New Zealand.

Some springtails can survive being frozen solid for years! They are tiny, ice-dwelling insects that feed on bits of food carried up by the wind.

**Fuji:** Japanese macaque monkey; **Kilimanjaro:** mountain reedbuck; **Mauna Loa:** human!

# Mountain Spirits

Mountain peaks, shrouded in cloud, have aroused fear and wonder for thousands of years. Before people could reach the summits, because of the steep slopes and terrible weather, they believed that only spirits and gods could live up that high. A few people who managed to scale the slopes brought back stories of strange tracks in the snow, eerie screams and wails, and monsters half glimpsed among the rocks.

## Lord of the Mountains

In ancient times, people depended on nature for food, shelter, and other needs. To give thanks, they made natural features and living things into gods and lords and worshipped them. For the ancient Japanese, the Lord of the Mountains was the bear that once roamed their land. It provided meat, fur, skins, and medicines. Each winter, people honored it with the Bear Festival, to persuade it to look kindly on their winter hunts.

## A perfect peak

Japan's highest mountain, the volcano Mount Fuji at 12,388 feet (3,778m), is an almost perfect cone shape. In clear weather, the five lakes around its base beautifully reflect its slopes and peak. Sometimes the snowy summit rises above the clouds, or the entire mountain eerily disappears in mist. Until the 1700s, the crater regularly spewed fire and lava.

When Mount Fuji erupted in ancient times, people believed that the mountain gods were punishing them for their sins.

Legends galore: **Everest:** Himalayas, home to the Abominable Snowman or yeti.

# Sacred inspiration

Because of its size, beauty, and power, Fuji is the most sacred place in Japan. Through the ages it has inspired writers, poets, artists, and musicians. Every summer, thousands of pilgrims climb through the night to pray, leave offerings, and watch the sunrise from the holy summit, which purifies their souls.

This *torri*, or ritual archway, is among the dark volcanic rocks on the summit of Mount Fuji. It is studded with coins left as gifts to the gods.

# Mountain monkeys

Legend tells how the mountain macaque monkeys came to Japan even before the first people. Today the main Japanese religions, Shinto and Buddhism, still hold sacred all forms of life. Some Shinto followers worship the macaques as messengers of the mountain gods. And the monkeys' silly antics also amuse countless climbers and tourists.

Macaque monkeys keep warm in the hot springs of Japan's highlands.

## Home of the gods

Mount Olympus, in northern Greece, rises 9,570 feet (2,919m) into the sky. Ancient Greeks believed that the summit, the highest place in their land, was home to their gods. The Greeks told stories of how their gods fought, lived, and loved, way above the clouds, unseen by ordinary humans. Each god and goddess watched over one aspect of the world. The great Zeus, father of the Olympian gods, ruled them all.

This ancient Greek carving shows the chief god Zeus, Hera his wife, and his twin children, daughter Artemis and son Apollo, on Mount Olympus.

**Aconcagua:** Sun gods; **Fuji:** a Shinto holy place; **Mauna Loa:** fire gods spat flames.

# Mountain People

Life on the high slopes is tough, with rugged terrain, little food, and severe weather. Many mountain people are largely cut off from their neighbors, since travel and trade are difficult. They must cope with harsh conditions and provide their own food and shelter. But there are advantages. Sheltered high valleys have fertile soil and plentiful running water. And they are well protected from hostile invasions.

## Pastures new

The Masai are wandering people who live on the lowlands, in the shadows of mountains such as Kilimanjaro, in Africa. As the hot, dry season parches the grassy lowlands, the Masai and their cattle move to the foothills for water and fresh grazing. The cattle provide almost every need, including the Masai's main foods—milk and blood. The animals are even used as a form of money. In the Himalayas, similarly, yaks provide meat, furs, and skins for leather. In the Andes, llamas and alpacas are used in the same way.

## Human transport

One of the highest countries in the world is Nepal, in the Himalayas. The land is so rough that there are few roads. Even pack animals like yaks cannot transport goods on the steepest mountain paths. So people have to carry their own food, water, clothes, and other items to the highest villages. The Nepalese Sherpas are experts at this and famed as mountain guides and porters.

Mountain porters, or Sherpas, are skilled at finding their way and surviving in mountains.

Nearby big cities: **Everest**: Lhasa of Tibet, 12,086 feet (3,686m), world's highest capital;

In the Annapurna area of Nepal, the sun sets on terraced strip fields of rice plants on the steep mountainsides.

## Terraced fields

Even today, many Nepalese people live isolated in high mountain valleys. Tall peaks block out radio and television signals. But rugged roads, railroads and small airstrips allow some travel and trade with India, China, and Bangladesh. Nepalese farmers grow herbs, grains, and vegetables using terraces – strips of level, fertile soil held in place by walls along the hillside.

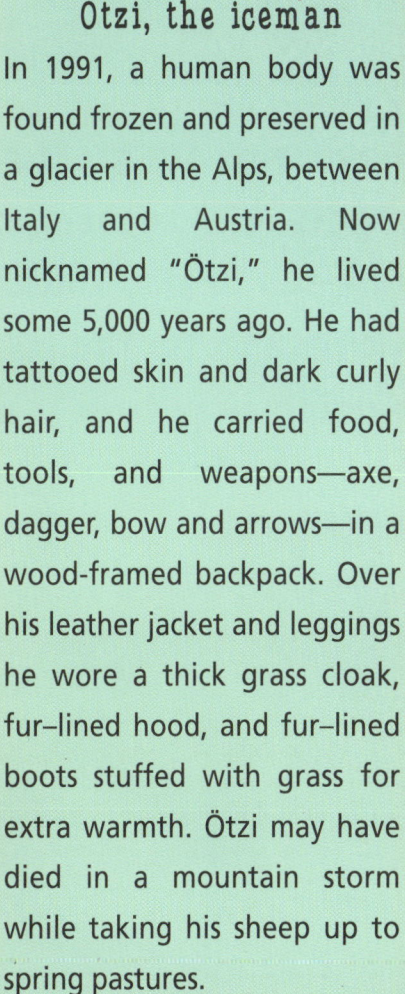

### Otzi, the iceman

In 1991, a human body was found frozen and preserved in a glacier in the Alps, between Italy and Austria. Now nicknamed "Ötzi," he lived some 5,000 years ago. He had tattooed skin and dark curly hair, and he carried food, tools, and weapons—axe, dagger, bow and arrows—in a wood-framed backpack. Over his leather jacket and leggings he wore a thick grass cloak, fur-lined hood, and fur-lined boots stuffed with grass for extra warmth. Ötzi may have died in a mountain storm while taking his sheep up to spring pastures.

## Government and roads

By the fifteenth century, the empire of the Incas included most of the Andes. Their dwellings had thick stone walls to protect against the bitter cold. The deserted Inca city of Machu Picchu is on a steep cliff 7,874 feet (2,402m) high on Mount Ausangate, Peru. The massive stone blocks were cut precisely, moved from quarries across the mountains, and positioned accurately for building—all without machines!

The ruins of Machu Picchu nestle among the Andean crags.

**Aconcagua:** Santiago; **Kilimanjaro:** Nairobi; **Mauna Loa:** Honolulu; **Fuji:** Tokyo.

# Fun in the Mountains

Mountains are great places to "get away from it all." There's spectacular scenery, clean fresh air, pretty flowers, and unusual animals, peaks, and cliffs to climb, and snow for skiing and other winter sports. The main drawback is that many other people are getting away from it all, too!

## The challenge to climb

Why risk life and limb to climb the world's tallest peaks? The usual reply is: "Because they're there!" The idea of being the first to stand on a summit began in Europe.

The highest alpine mountain, Mont Blanc at 15,771 feet (4,807m), was climbed in 1786. Most other European peaks were soon conquered. Climbers improved their methods and equipment, and turned to North and South America and Africa for new challenges. Yet it was only in the 1950s that they scaled the greatest peaks of all—those in the Himalayas.

## Safety first

Today's mountaineers use very strong man-made materials for their ropes, clips, harnesses, and lightweight, weatherproof clothing. Experts can teach climbing and other mountain skills in safe places with artificial climbing walls and ski slopes. Then people can attempt the real thing. Despite all the training and precautions, there are always risks.

**Kilimanjaro:** first climbed in 1889; **Aconcagua:** in 1897; **Everest:** in 1953.

Skiing downhill is exciting and exhilarating. Skiing uphill is far more tiring, and most people take the cable car!

## Rapid descent

Various kinds of skiing, from cross-country (Nordic) to downhill (Alpine) and ski jumping, are big business in mountain resorts all over the world. Newer offshoots of skiing include snowboarding and snowshoeing, while bobsledding and tobogganing are also fast ways of getting down a snowy slope. These sports bring much money to the local communities in mountain regions.

## Best in the winter world

Winter sports such as ice-skating, ice hockey, and curling are played when the weather is cold enough for water to freeze. Every four years, the best sports people gather somewhere mountainous for the Winter Olympics. In the summer or in warmer regions people go hill walking, rock climbing, abseiling, hang gliding, paragliding, and even ballooning.

### On the top of the world

The world's tallest mountain, Everest, was first scaled by New Zealand climber Edmund Hillary on May 29, 1953 and Nepalese Sherpa guide Norgay Tenzing. They left behind a crucifix, and a bar of chocolate as an offering to Buddhist gods. But great feats of mountaineering continued. The following year, an Italian team led by Ardito Desio finally conquered treacherous K2, the world's second highest mountain measuring 28,251 feet (8,611m) in height.

Tenzing and Hillary leave Camp 8 on their way to the top.

**Mauna Loa:** many visitors come to witness the great spectacle of a volcanic eruption.

# Mountain Riches

Because conditions are so harsh, and transportation is difficult, there are few heavy industries and little mining in most mountain regions. But this is gradually changing, as resources elsewhere run low and machines and vehicles become more powerful.

Grain is ground into flour for bread, in Bhutan, Himalayas.

## Crops for food and cash

Despite the cool, windy conditions on many mountains, people manage to grow some crops. The Andean Indians cultivate maize, wheat, and potatoes for themselves, and sugar, rice, and coffee mainly for export. Some have been lured or bullied into growing illegal drug crops, such as coca (which yields cocaine) or poppies (for opium), in remote valleys. The mountains shield their unlawful plantations.

## Mountain minerals

The world's industries depend on huge supplies of fuels and minerals such as coal and sulfur. These occur in rocks—and mountains are made of rocks. But extracting them is difficult, and therefore expensive, in mountainous regions.

However, it is sometimes worth mining mountains for precious metals like gold and silver and for gems such as diamonds and rubies. Ancient South Americans worshipped gold because it shone bright yellow, like the sun. Using only stone tools, they dug tons of it from the Andes and fashioned it into beautiful jewelery and ornaments.

However, most of the easily-mined reserves of fuels and minerals in the lowlands have been used up. Mountain railroads and truck roads are driving ever higher into the highlands.

**Mauna Loa**: nearby Mauna Kea is home to the world's largest telescope.

# Mountain metals

Today, some mountains are mined for important metals needed by modern industry. In the Chilean Andes, copper ore is blasted from the mountainsides with dynamite, leaving massive holes. Nitrate minerals, used as fertilizer, are extracted by pumping water through rocks to dissolve them. The Andes also yield tin, lead, zinc, and antimony.

Mining for metals, such as copper and tin, destroys the natural wildlife and leaves vast open scars on the landscape.

## African diamond mines

One of the world's most valuable minerals is the diamond, treasured for its beauty, and also by industry for its incredible hardness. Diamonds were created by the same extraordinary forces of temperature and pressure that built mountains such as Kilimanjaro. The gems occur deep in seams of cooled volcanic lava, in places such as Kimberley, South Africa. Legend says that the wealth and power of ancient Israel's King Solomon came from his secret diamond mines in Africa.

# Mountain power

Another mountain resource is the energy of water flowing downhill, from the snow and glaciers of the heights. All over the world, people exploit this energy. They build dams to channel the water past huge fanlike turbine blades, which spin around and generate electricity. In mountainous countries such as Norway and New Zealand, nine-tenths of electricity is made in this way.

Hydroelectricity is produced from water held back by dams.

**Kilimanjaro:** tourists can trek to the summit, but at nearly 20,000 feet (6,000m), it's a hard climb.

# Preserving our Peaks

All over the world, natural places are being destroyed and damaged. Mountains are remote and inaccessible, but they too are beginning to suffer. Farmers and hunters have forced animals such as bears and wolves up to the highest, most hostile peaks. But even these places are affected by climbers, miners, bikers, tourists, and travelers, and the worn paths, roads, buildings, litter, and pollution they bring.

## Mountaintop garbage tip

Every year more tourists climb to the top of Mount Fuji in Japan. It is supposed to be a place of cleanliness and purity. But often they find drinks cans, candy wrappers, and other trash. The same happens on many other mountains. Visitors wear away paths, make noise, pick wild flowers and disturb animals—destroying the very features that attracted them in the first place.

There's no easy answer. Many people do not see why they should have to pay, or be kept on small paths, in these wild, free places.

Plastic bags, cans, papers, and packages litter a mountain rest site. It's unsightly, and also a danger to inquisitive animals.

## Disappearing mountain

Mount Fuji and similar peaks near built-up areas are under more threats. They are eroding faster than ever because of acid rain caused by pollution. This is produced by fumes from power stations, vehicles, factories, and fires. The strongly acidic chemicals eat into the rock and turn it into rubble.

**Everest** has about 12,000 visitors a year, limited only by the capacity of its tiny airports.

# Washed away

Another great threat is logging—for mountains, and lowlands, too. Valuable trees high on the slopes are cut down for timber. But as they are dragged away, the hillsides lose their protection. The next rains wash the loose soil down to the rivers. This means the mountainsides are bare and rocky, empty of wildlife, while the lowland rivers choke with mud and silt. Vast areas of Bangladesh, India, and Pakistan suffer great floods due to logging and poor farming on the slopes of the Himalayas.

Uncontrolled logging has devastated this Himalayan hillside and its wildlife. Such damage will last for a century or more.

## Mountain gorillas

There are only a few hundred mountain gorillas left in the world, in the uplands of Rwanda and Zaïre, in Africa. These gentle but powerful animals are found only in forests above 5,251 feet (1,600m). But they are threatened by loggers and farmers who destroy their habitat, by poachers who sell their body parts as trophies, and by warring groups who battle for control of the region. Even high in the mountains they are not safe.

Mountain gorillas are among the world's most endangered creatures.

Should the government try to reduce the number of tourists to protect the environment?

# Glossary

**altitude** How high something is, usually its height above the sea's average level.

**block–fault mountains** Mountains formed when a huge block of rock, between two cracks, or faults, in Earth's surface, rises upward due to Earth's movements.

**climate** General pattern of weather conditions in an area over a long time—years and centuries.

**condense** When a gas or vapor turns into a liquid as it cools.

**conservation** Preserving or keeping something in its original condition.

**continental drift** Slow, gradual movements of the huge landmasses around Earth, due to movements of the lithospheric plates, which carry them.

**crust** Earth's "skin," the relatively thin outer, solid layer of rock that floats on the hot liquid mantle beneath.

**deciduous trees** Trees that lose or shed their leaves at certain times of the year.

**earthquake** Sudden, violent shaking of Earth's surface due to abrupt movements of the lithospheric plates.

**equator** An imaginary line around Earth's widest part, halfway between the Poles.

**erosion** Gradual breaking down and wearing away of rocks or other substances.

**fault** Deep crack in Earth's rocky crust.

**fold mountains** Mountains formed by the folding or buckling of Earth's rocky crust, due to movements of the lithospheric plates.

**glacier** Mass of ice, usually long and ribbon shaped, that creeps or flows slowly downward from high ground.

**hydroelectric power** Electricity generated by the flow of water, usually through a dam across a river.

**lava** Incredibly hot, melted, or molten rock that erupts from volcanoes.

**lithosphere** Layer of rocks that covers Earth's surface, made of the solid crust plus the outer, part-melted layer of the mantle below.

**lithospheric plates** Massive jigsaw-like slabs of rock, which make up the lithosphere, and which move or slide to cause continental drift.

**mantle** Very thick, hot, part-melted layer of rock, beneath Earth's crust and around its central core.

**migrate** Move from one region or climate usually on regular there-and-back journeys with the changing seasons.

**minerals** Natural substances, often formed as crystals, which make up Earth's rocks. There are more than 3,000 types.

**molten** When a normally solid substance is so hot, it melts into a liquid.

**ore** Rocks and rocky materials that are rich in useful substances, like metals such as iron, gold, or copper, or minerals such as sulfur.

**orogeny** Mountain building.

**pollution** Contamination by harmful, unsightly, or unnatural substances, such as piles of garbage or industrial chemicals in air or soil.

**rain shadow** Area where rain rarely falls, because the winds have lost their moisture.

**resource** Useful substance.

**strata** Layers of sedimentary rocks.

**terracing** Creating level strip-shaped farm fields on mountainsides, by building step-like shelves.

**tropical** In the belt of land and sea around Earth's middle, to either side of the equator, where the climate is mostly hot and damp.

**volcano** Mountain created by lava pushed through a hole or crack in Earth's crust.

**water vapor** Invisible type of gas formed when water gets warm and evaporates.

**weathering** When heat, cold, rain, ice, wind, and other natural forces wear away, or erode, like a mountain.

# Fact File

## Five highest mountains in the world

| NAME | RANGE | LOCATION | HEIGHT |
|---|---|---|---|
| Everest | Himalayas | Nepal | 29,035 feet (8,850m) |
| K2 | Himalayas | Kashmir | 28,248 feet (8,610m) |
| Kangchenjunga | Himalayas | Nepal | 28,182 feet (8,590m) |
| Lhotse | Himalayas | Nepal | 27,887 feet (8,500m) |
| Makalu | Himalayas | Nepal | 27,788 feet (8,470m) |

(The top 28 highest peaks in the world are in the Himalayas)

## Other highest mountains (in order)

**SOUTH AMERICA**
Aconcagua, Andes, Argentina — 22,831 feet (6,959m)

**NORTH AMERICA**
McKinley, Alaskan, Alaska — 20,321 feet (6,194m)
Elbert, Rockies, Colorado — 14,432 feet (4,399m)

**AFRICA**
Kilimanjaro, isolated, Tanzania — 19,340 feet (5,895m)

**ANTARCTICA**
Vinson — 16,863 feet (5,140m)

**EUROPE**
Blanc, European Alps, France/Italy — 15,771 feet (4,807m)

**OCEANIA**
Wilhelm, Papua New Guinea — 14,793 feet (4,509m)

**AUSTRALIA AND NEW ZEALAND**
Cook, Cook, New Zealand — 12,349 feet (3,764m)
Kosciusko, Australian Alps — 7,313 feet (2,229m)

## Highest extinct volcano
Aconcagua, above

## Highest active volcano
Popocatepetl, Mexico, at 17,989 feet (5,483m)

## Largest active volcano
Mauna Loa, Hawaii

## When mountains were built

4,600 million years ago (mya) Precambrian era
Earth's crust forms

3,800 (mya)
Oldest known rocks formed in Greenland. Mountains are built and eroded over the next 3,000 million years. Most of the world's rocks formed during this time

700 (mya)
Intense period of mountain building

500 (mya) Cambrian period
Major volcanic activity occurs in North America

410 (mya), Silurian period
New mountain ranges form

375 (mya) Devonian period
Continents collide and Caledonians and Urals form

300 (mya) Carboniferous period
Altai Mountains of Russia and Asia

250 (mya) Permian period
Appalachians of North America

230 (mya) Triassic period
A huge supercontinent, called Gondwanaland, breaks up to form the continents we have now

165 (mya) Jurassic period (dinosaurs rule)
Atlas mountains of North Africa begin to form

100 (mya) Cretaceous period
The Rockies in North America and the Andes in South America begin to form

50 (mya) Tertiary period
East Africa Rift Valley begins to open up, Kilimanjaro and mountains of East Africa form

40 (mya) Alps and Himalayas begin to form

25 (mya) Time of massive erosion

5 (mya) Andes begin second phase of uplift

# Index

acid rain 12, 28
Aconcagua 4, 6, 7, 10, 11, 14, 16, 19, 21, 24, 28, 31
Alps 5, 7, 19, 23, 24, 31
Altai Mountains 10, 31
Andes 5, 7, 10, 11, 12, 16, 17, 19, 22, 23, 26, 27, 31
animals 16–19, 20, 21, 22, 28, 29
Antarctica 13, 31
Atlas Mountains 5, 31

birds 16, 17, 18, 19
Blanc, Mount 24, 31
block-fault mountains 6, 11

Caledonian Mountains 10, 31
Cambrian Mountains 10
Chimborazo, Mount 5
climate *see* weather zones 16–17, 18
cloud forest 17
continental drift 6, 7
Cook, Mount 9, 31
crust, Earth's 6, 7, 8, 10, 31
   movements in 6, 7

Desio, Ardito 25
diamonds 26, 27

earthquakes 7, 8
erosion 7, 10, 28; *see also* weathering
Everest, Mount 4, 5, 6, 10, 11, 12, 14, 16, 19, 20, 22, 24, 25, 26, 28, 31

faults 6
fold mountains 6, 7, 8
frost wedging 13
Fuji, Mount 5, 9, 13, 14, 17, 20, 21, 23, 28, 29

gemstones 7; *see also* diamonds
glaciers 12, 13, 23
gold 7, 26

Hawaii 5, 9, 17, 31
Hillary, Edmund 25
Himalayas 4, 5, 7, 10, 11, 12, 16, 18, 19, 20, 22, 24, 26, 29, 31
hot spots 9
hydroelectricity 26, 27

ice 10, 12, 13, 15, 16, 17
iceman 23
Incas 23
insects 17, 18, 19

K2  25, 31
Karakoram Range 4
Kilimanjaro 5, 9, 13, 15, 16, 20, 22, 24, 27, 29, 31
Kosciusko 5, 31

lava 8, 11, 20, 27
lithospheric plates 6, 7, 8, 9

magma 8
mantle, Earth's 6, 9, 11
Mars 5
Matterhorn 11
Mauna Kea 9, 24
Mauna Loa 5, 8, 15, 16, 20, 21, 24, 29, 31
McKinley, Mount 15
metals 7, 26, 27
minerals 24, 27
mining 26–27
Mons Olympus 5
mountain people 22–23
mountain spirits 20–21

natural resources 7, 26–27

oceanic ridges 6
Olympus, Mount 21
orogeny 10

Pikes Peak 7
Pinatubo, Mount 9
plants 13, 16-17, 18
pollution 12, 28

rain, effects of 10, 13, 14
rain forests 16
rain shadow 14, 15
rivers 10, 11, 12
rocks 6, 7, 8, 10–11, 26
Rocky Mountains (Rockies) 5, 7, 15, 17, 31

sea mounts 9
sediments 11
Sherpas 22, 25
snow 13, 14

temperature 14–15, 16
Tenzing, Norgay 25
tourists/tourism 7, 21, 23, 24–25, 27, 28
trees 16, 17, 18, 29

Vinson Massif 13, 31
volcanoes 4, 5, 8–9, 11, 20, 27, 31

weather/weathering 10–13, 14–15, 22
wildlife 16-17, 27
winds 14-15, 16
winter sports 25

DATE DUE